country

flowers

Published by

Tesco Stores Limited

Created by Brilliant Books Ltd

84-86 Regent Street

London W1B 5RR

www.brilliantbooks.co.uk

First published 2001

Text and photographs © 2001 Brilliant Books Ltd

Reproduction by Colourpath, England

Printed by Artes Graficas Toledo, Spain

DLTO: 1629-2000

ISBN 1-84221-141-2

10 9 8 7 6 5 4 3 2 1

country

flowers

contents

introduction   7

techniques   8

spring flowers   **10**

summer flowers   **18**

autumn flowers   **30**

winter flowers   **40**

flower-holders   48

foliage   50

colour   52

context   54

glossary   56

index   62

photographs by **John Bellars**

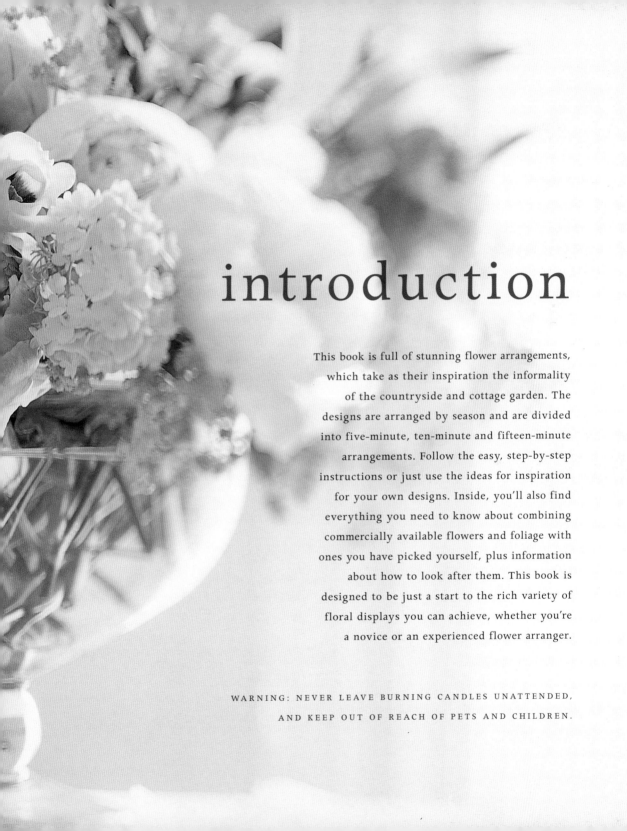

introduction

This book is full of stunning flower arrangements,
which take as their inspiration the informality
of the countryside and cottage garden. The
designs are arranged by season and are divided
into five-minute, ten-minute and fifteen-minute
arrangements. Follow the easy, step-by-step
instructions or just use the ideas for inspiration
for your own designs. Inside, you'll also find
everything you need to know about combining
commercially available flowers and foliage with
ones you have picked yourself, plus information
about how to look after them. This book is
designed to be just a start to the rich variety of
floral displays you can achieve, whether you're
a novice or an experienced flower arranger.

WARNING: NEVER LEAVE BURNING CANDLES UNATTENDED,
AND KEEP OUT OF REACH OF PETS AND CHILDREN.

Techniques

Some tips to help you when you come to do any of the arrangements in this book

RECOMMENDED
EQUIPMENT
- good-quality florist's scissors, sharp household scissors (used solely for flowers so as to prevent the spread of bacteria) or secateurs
- small knife
- garden string or raffia
- floral foam for wet flowers
- florist's wire
- florist's tape
- chickenwire

Cutting stems

Cut stems at an angle to create a larger surface area for water absorption. Always use sharp tools to make a clean cut. Place the stems in water as soon as possible after cutting or they will begin to seal over again. Spring flowers should have any white part of the stem removed, as this will not take up water. Woody stems should be split several centimetres up the base. Carnations should be cut above or below the hard node or swelling in the stem, as they will not take up water if you cut through this.

Removing foliage

Using just your hands, strip from the stems any foliage that will lie below the waterline. Try not to damage the stem, as that would allow bacteria to infect it. Carefully remove thorns with a knife.

Feeding

Add commercial flower-food to clean, tepid water, according to the instructions on the packet.

Straightening stems

Some flowers, such as tulips, have a tendency to droop. To straighten the stems, wrap them in paper and secure with adhesive tape, recut the stems and place in clean water with flower food for spring flowers for several hours.

Reviving roses

Sometimes the stems of roses become blocked with air bubbles, which makes them drop their heads. Wrap them in damp paper, cover their heads for protection and cut several centimetres from their stems. Plunge the stems into warm water for 45 minutes and then into clean, deep, cold water with flower food to recover.

Removing stamens

To prevent the pollen from some lilies staining clothes or tablecloths, remove the stamens.

Topping up with water

Top up with clean water every two or three days. Mist cut flowers with water to prevent water loss.

Using floral foam

Cover floral foam with water until it floats, then leave it to absorb water at its own rate. Don't push the foam underwater, as this may create air pockets. Never let foam dry out – it will not absorb water properly again. And don't re-use it.

one

Heaven scent

With their beautiful flowers and heady fragrance, hyacinths need only the simplest of arrangements

one Fill the jug with water. Don't cut the hyacinth stems as the bulbous ends contain a small amount of food. Place the stems in the water, with the ceanothus if you are using it.

other ideas Anemones look lovely in a small jug, as do lilac or sweet peas, which both have the bonus of a wonderful scent.

WHAT YOU NEED

- 8–10 hyacinths (depending on the size of your jug)
- 5 stems of ceanothus, cut from your garden (optional)
- small ceramic jug

TOP TIP
Keep the hyacinths in a cool place and they should last for ten days.

one

two

thre

Spring sunshine

Celebrate the end of winter with this dazzling display of narcissi and pussy willow

one Fill the vase with water and add the beads.

two Add the viburnum, placing the shorter stems around the edge of the bowl and the longer ones in the middle – they will help to support the stems of the narcissi.

three Position the narcissi in small groups in between the viburnum stems. Finally, add the stems of pussy willow.

other ideas You could substitute wax flowers and grape hyacinths for the narcissi, but you would have to use a smaller bowl.

WHAT YOU NEED

- 40 narcissi (2 different varieties)
- 8 stems of viburnum of various lengths
- 8 stems of pussy willow, cut to different lengths
- medium-sized glass fish-bowl vase
- 2 handfuls of clear glass beads (available from department stores)

TOP TIP

Place flowers in groups – it creates a stronger and more natural design.

one   two

Herb garden

Here's a novel way of keeping your culinary herbs tidy and adding colour to your kitchen

one Transfer the herbs from their plastic containers to more stylish terracotta pots and place them in the wooden box.

two Fill the glasses with water and place a small bunch of anemones in each glass. Position the glasses between the herb pots.

other ideas You could use hyacinths for a fragrant alternative, or spray carnations.

WHAT YOU NEED
- 25 anemones in a variety of colours
- 4 pots of culinary herbs
- 4 terracotta pots
- wooden box or crate
- 4 glasses

TOP TIP
Anemones have a tendency to lean towards the light, so keep them in an evenly lit area or turn them occasionally.

one

two

three

Touching tulips

Taking the time to make this gift for Mother's Day or Easter will really add to the pleasure it gives

one Line the box with the tissue paper. Tie raffia or ribbon around the box for decoration.

two Place the watertight container in the centre of the tissue paper and fill with water.

three Cut some of the tulips slightly shorter than the others. Position the tulips in the container in colour or texture groups – this creates a stronger design. Form a natural dome by placing the shorter stems closer to the edge and the longer ones towards the centre.

other ideas Try using daffodils or irises.

WHAT YOU NEED

- 25 tulips (2–3 different varieties)
- decorative box or container about 15cm (6in) square (it doesn't have to be watertight)
- 4 sheets of coloured tissue paper
- raffia or ribbon
- watertight container to fit inside the box

TOP TIP

Cut tulips a little shorter than other flowers, as they continue growing after they have been cut.

one

two

Eastern promise

Give your living room a Japanese air with elegant oriental lilies and tortured willow

one Trim the foam, then place it in the bowl.
two Fix the tortured willow stems in the foam. Cut the lily stem down, removing two open flowers and two buds. Position the open flowers at the base of the arrangement, then set the two buds and stem in place.

other ideas Nerines (Guernsey lilies) or orchids both impart a similarly oriental mood.

WHAT YOU NEED

- 1 stem of oriental lilies
- 3 stems of tortured willow, available from florists
- small oriental-style bowl
- floral foam for wet flowers, pre-soaked

TOP TIP

Don't overcrowd this arrangement – it is very important to keep it simple.

Rose-tinted glasses

Instead of having a central table-decoration, give all your guests their very own flower arrangement

WHAT YOU NEED
- 1 small rose for each place-setting
- 1 champagne flute for each place-setting
- stems of trailing ivy

one Fill the flutes with water. Cut each rose stem to a length of 20cm (8in) and place a single stem in each glass. Repeat at each place-setting.

other ideas Mini-gerberas (germinis) create a fun look, while orchids are more sophisticated.

one

two

Berries and cream

Nothing could evoke summertime better than a combination of strawberries and fragrant stocks

one Fill the jug with water and add the gypsophila in clumps of two or three stems.
two Cut the stocks to varying heights and thread them through the gypsophila for support.
three Place the jug on the plate and then scatter the summer fruits around it.

other ideas For a different colour scheme you could use scabious instead of the stocks, sedum instead of the gypsophila, and blueberries, blackcurrants and blackberries.

WHAT YOU NEED
- 10 stems of cream and white stocks
- 10 stems of gypsophila
- cream ceramic jug
- cream ceramic plate
- various summer fruits

TOP TIP
Whenever you combine flowers with fruit, make sure the fruit is very fresh – as it ripens it emits ethylene, which can damage flowers.

 one
 two
 thre

Traditional trug

This display gives the illusion of flowers just picked from the garden, gathered in a basket

one Line the basket with the plastic to prevent water from leaking out. Place the floral foam inside and trim away any excess plastic.

two Cut the bupleurum into short branches and insert in the foam – they should all face towards one end of the basket and look as though they are lying flat.

three Cut the asters into short stems and add with the freesias in the same direction as the foliage. Insert any discarded stems in the other end of the foam to complete the illusion.

WHAT YOU NEED
- 10 stems of pink freesias
- 3 stems of asters
- 3–4 stems of summer foliage, such as bupleurum
- wooden trug or flat basket
- plastic for lining, such as part of a bin-liner
- 30cm x 10cm (12in x 4in) piece of floral foam for wet flowers, pre-soaked

TOP TIP
Top up the foam with water frequently.

one

two

thre

Rural romance

This charming arrangement makes a wonderful display for a special occasion such as a wedding

one Fill the bowl two-thirds full with water. Using the tape, make a grid across the top of the bowl to support the flowers. Make sure you stick down the tape well.

two Cut the lady's mantle into stems of 10–15cm (4–6in) in length and place in the grid in groups of two or three to create a dome shape.

three Cut the peonies, spray roses, lisianthus and viburnum opulus into stems of 10–15cm (4–6in) in length. Add the flowers in groups, starting at the edge of the bowl and working towards the centre.

WHAT YOU NEED

- 8–10 peonies
- 3 stems of lady's mantle
- 3 stems of spray roses
- 2 stems of lisianthus
- 2–3 stems of viburnum opulus
- glass bowl (preferably on a stand)
- clear adhesive tape

TOP TIPS

This arrangement enables stems to absorb the optimal amount of water, which is very important for delicate flowers such as peonies.

one
two
thre

Flower show

This tree-shaped design can be made with many varieties of flower and in different sizes

one Tie the sticks together with the string or fine rope and position in the terracotta pot. Fill the pot with pebbles to hold the sticks upright.

two Press the foam on the sticks. Cut the foliage into lengths of 12.5–15cm (5–6in) and insert it in the foam to create an arrangement of the shape and size you desire.

three Cut chrysanthemums down into short stems and add in groups of two or three stems of the same colour. Insert the ivy in the bottom of the foam and trail around the sticks.

WHAT YOU NEED

- 15 stems of spray chrysanthemums in three colours
- 4 stems of variegated foliage, such as euonymus
- 1 stem of trailing ivy
- large terracotta pot
- 3 sticks or canes (or 1 thicker one)
- garden string or fine rope
- 10cm x 7.5cm (4in x 3in) piece of floral foam for wet flowers, pre-soaked and with its corners trimmed
- small pebbles

one

two

thr

Wild bunch

Birch twigs help keep the flowers in place and make just a few stems go a long way

one Divide the twigs into small bundles, reserving a few to go in the container with the flowers. Bind each bundle with florist's wire — you may need to do this in several places.

two Attach the twig bundles to the basket with more wire, poking it through the basket and twisting to hold it loosely in place.

three Place the watertight container in the basket and fill with water. Place the remaining twigs in the container and thread the stems of flowers through them.

WHAT YOU NEED
- 7 stems of lilac and white lisianthus
- about 20 birch twigs (available from florists or in your garden)
- basket
- watertight container that fits inside the basket
- florist's wire

TOP TIP
If you want to reuse the birch twigs that have been in water, rinse them well.

one

two

thre

Floral harvest

Create a rustic effect by using fabric to cover a flowerpot and chickenwire to hold the flowers

one Wrap the flowerpot with the material and tie the cord or ribbon around it.

two Sit the watertight container in the flowerpot, then scrunch up the chickenwire and place it in the container. Fill with water.

three Start by inserting the foliage through the gaps in the wire. Add the flowers to create an informal, natural-looking dome shape.

other ideas A ready-arranged mixed autumn bouquet is ideal for this design.

WHAT YOU NEED

- 6 stems of celosia (2 different types)
- 4–5 stems of crocosmia
- 3 stems of antirrhinums
- 2 stems of mini-chrysanthemums
- 5–6 stems of seasonal foliage, such as privet
- flowerpot
- material
- cord or ribbon to tie
- watertight container, which should fit tightly inside the flowerpot
- a 30cm x 30cm (12in x 12in) piece of chickenwire

one

two

three

Autumnal roses

After the blaze of summer is over, berries and late-flowering roses still provide vibrant colour

one Line the urn with plastic to stop any water leaking out. Cut the foam to fit, place it in the urn and trim away any excess plastic.

two Cut the rose stems so that they are 5–6cm (2–2½in) long. Insert the roses in the foam in groups of three. Add the berries in between.

three Cut the ivy into short stems and position them in the foam towards the bottom of the arrangement.

other ideas You could try carnations and spray carnations with just a few roses.

WHAT YOU NEED

- 10 roses (2 different colours)
- 3 stems of hypericum berries
- 2 stems of viburnum berries
- 1 stem of trailing ivy
- cast-iron or ceramic urn
- plastic lining
- floral foam for wet flowers, pre-soaked

TOP TIP

Keep the foam topped up with water and the roses should last for seven days.

 one
 two
 three

Hand-tied bouquet

This is a lovely way of arranging flowers to give to someone, and is not as difficult as it looks

one Strip the foliage from the lower half of the stems. Lay out everything in front of you.

two Starting with a single stem held loosely between your thumb and index finger, add more stems into your hand at a slight angle, turning the bouquet as you add each new stem to form a spiral in your hand and a flat dome of flowers.

three Tie the raffia or string loosely around the stems, about a third of the way up. Trim the stems. Fold each sheet of tissue paper in half to form two triangles. Wrap a sheet around each side of the bouquet and tie with raffia or string.

WHAT YOU NEED

- 2–3 stems of alstroemeria (Peruvian lilies)
- 2 stems of carthamus
- 6 stems of rudbeckia
- 3–4 stems of achillea
- 6 poppy heads
- 2 stems of hypericum berries
- raffia or garden string
- 2 sheets of tissue paper

TOP TIP

Leave the tie on when you place the flowers in a vase to keep the bouquet intact.

one

two

thre

Harvest festival

Incorporating vegetables in this display helps to evoke the mellow fruitfulness of autumn

one Cut the top off the pumpkin and discard the seeds. Line with the plastic and place the floral foam inside. Trim away the excess plastic.

two Cut the lily stems down so you end up with individual flowers. Insert the stems of the sedum and lilies in the foam.

three Use raffia to bind the vegetables on to wooden skewers and then stick them in the foam.

other ideas Chrysanthemums in autumn colours also work well in this arrangement.

WHAT YOU NEED

- 3 stems of asiatic lilies in two different colours
- 3–4 stems of sedum
- medium pumpkin
- various vegetables, such as peppers, garlic, mini-carrots, mangetout and spring onions
- thick plastic for lining
- block of floral foam for wet flowers 25cm x 10cm (10in x 4in), pre-soaked
- raffia
- wooden cocktail skewers or cocktail sticks

one

Winter white

This arrangement makes the most of a few blooms at a time when flowers are more expensive

one Fill the jug with water. Mass the eucalyptus and viburnum together and place in the jug to form a framework for the display – the narrow neck of the jug will help.

two Thread the stems of the eryngium through the foliage and add the white roses for a subtle contrast. If you have any flowers or foliage left over, cut the stems short and place them in two ceramic bowls close to the jug.

other ideas Using a few gerberas instead of the roses looks equally effective.

WHAT YOU NEED
- 2 stems of eryngium
- 8–12 white roses
- 5–6 stems of eucalyptus
- 2 stems of viburnum
- tall jug or similar container
- 2 small ceramic bowls, (optional)

TOP TIP
Keep this arrangement very informal – it should look as if the stems have just been gathered together.

one

two

Christmas spray

This sweet way to make a gift look extra-special can decorate a box, bottle or mirror, too

one Cut the foliage and thistle into short stems. Insert a few stems in the foam dome to form the shape of a cross.

two Continue adding the foliage and thistles. Tie the ribbon round two stems to form loops.

three Finish by placing the rose in the centre of the spray and use the self-adhesive pad on the foam dome to attach it to the gift.

other ideas Any small sprigs of foliage and left-over flowers can be used for these decorations. You could also use dried flowers.

WHAT YOU NEED

- 1 rose
- 1 stem of echinops thistle, cut into short stems
- 1 stem of holly
- 1 stem of ivy
- 1 stem of rosemary
- self-adhesive floral foam dome 4cm (1 $\frac{1}{2}$ in) in diameter, pre-soaked for one minute (available from florists)
- 2 lengths of the ribbon used to wrap the present

one

two

Foliage swag

**This scented Christmas decoration looks
equally good hung on a door or window**

one Strip the leaves from the lower stems
of the foliage, then bunch the stems together,
splaying them to form a fan shape.

two Continue to add the foliage in groups.
Tie the stems firmly together near the base with
raffia or string and finish with a ribbon bow.

other ideas A single variety of foliage, such
as eucalyptus, also works well.

WHAT YOU NEED
- 2 stems of viburnum
- 2 stems of pine
- 5–6 stems of eucalyptus
- 5–6 stems of rosemary
- 2 stems of eryngium
- raffia or garden string
- decorative ribbon

TOP TIP
If you use a single variety
of foliage, spray it with
gold or silver paint for a
particularly festive look.

one

two

thre

Advent ring

Flowers, foliage and fir cones combine to make this traditional Christmas table-decoration

WARNING

Never leave unattended candles burning. Keep out of reach of children. Do not let the candles burn down too close to the dry fir cones, when they could become a fire hazard or cause damage to the surface the arrangement is on.

one Place the four candles securely in the floral foam ring to form a square, making sure they are secure. Cut the foliage into short lengths and add in small groups, making sure you cover the base completely.

two Twist florist's wire around the base of each of the fir cones and add in small clusters.

three Insert the individual amaryllis flowers in the foam, evenly spaced. Finish with groups of the carnations and spray carnations. Take care not to let the foam dry out.

WHAT YOU NEED

- 3-4 stems of amaryllis cut down into individual flowers
- 8-10 burgundy carnations
- 5–7 stems of burgundy spray carnations
- 6 stems of ruscus
- 2 stems of ming fern
- 32 fir cones
- floral foam ring for wet flowers 30–35cm (12in–14in) in diameter, pre-soaked
- 4 church candles
- strong florist's wire

Flower-holders

The type of container you use will affect the final appearance of your arrangement just as much as the flowers you choose

The container you choose should complement the flowers, rather than overshadow them. Try to keep the vase or holder as simple as possible – patterns will only complicate things.

Think about the setting in which you will be placing the arrangement – the surrounding colours and textures will give you clues for the most suitable container. The earthy colours and textures of pottery, baskets and wood give a very different look from the manufactured qualities of glass, metal and glossy ceramics.

You can create a container from items you might find around the house or in the garden. Even if the container itself isn't watertight, you can always stand inside it an inner container that is.

Whatever you choose, make sure that it is clean, as this affects how long the flowers last. Use a little bleach or general cleaner and rinse well.

Foliage

Foliage can be as crucial to a floral design as flowers

Today there are a vast number of different types of foliage available commercially and these will last longer than something cut from your garden.

Foliage should not just be a 'filler' – it should always enhance an arrangement and complement the flowers. Combine garden or country-style flowers with soft, flowing foliage such as pittosporum or bupleurum. Simple flowers look best with bear grass or palm leaves.

Tree fern

One of the large group of asparagus ferns, tree fern is very useful as a delicate filler. Although it looks very fragile, it will last for up to two weeks and is available all year round.

Bear grass

A long, fine grass that is used in contemporary arrangements to soften and give movement, bear grass is longlasting and can also be dried. It lasts for between ten days and two weeks.

Eucalyptus

A very popular foliage because of its aromatic scent, eucalyptus comes in a variety of different leaf shapes and shades. It can also be dried and sprayed. It lasts for ten days to two weeks.

Rosemary

Still relatively new to commercial production, rosemary is a great bonus in an arrangement because of its sweet fragrance. If you mist it with water, it will last for up to ten days.

Hard ruscus

Large glossy leaves spiralling down a short stem make this plant particularly longlasting. Soft ruscus has a longer, arching stem and thinner leaves. Both last for up to two weeks.

Sword fern

With its lime-green colour and elegant shape, sword fern can be used in many ways. If you mist it with water, it will last for seven to ten days.

Colour

Colour is a key factor to consider when choosing flowers, as it can create a variety of moods and effects

The colour wheel is made up of three primary colours (red, blue and yellow), three secondary colours (orange, green and violet) and tertiary colours, which are made by mixing a primary colour with its adjacent secondary colour. When putting different colours together in a flower arrangement, let one colour dominate and don't be afraid of using colour asymetrically.

Monochromatic colour scheme
This is a combination of shades of one colour, but can also include white. Blue and white produce a calming effect and are good for a bright bathroom or bedroom. Soft reds and pinks conjure a romantic mood for an intimate dinner.

Primary colours
Combining red, blue and yellow flowers creates a very bold, cheerful colour scheme that would be great for a party. You could make it subtler by using slightly toned-down shades.

Complementary colours

Here you use two colours that lie opposite each
other in the colour wheel. The best combinations
pair a primary colour with an opposite secondary
colour. Orange and blue, for example, is a lively,
attractive combination that would be good to
give to someone to cheer them up. Lime-green
with orange is a fresh, tangy partnership.

Harmonious colours

Colours that lie next to each other on the colour
wheel, such as yellow and green, blue and violet
and red and orange, are called harmonious colours.
They provide a subtle contrast in an arrangement.

Triadic colour scheme

This colour scheme uses three colours from the
different areas in the colour wheel. It may be
used in any combination and can produce some
unusual effects. For example, cerise, yellow
and orange give a tropical feeling.

Context

Taking care where you place flowers will ensure they look their best and last as long as possible

Flowers can add life and colour to every room in the house. Place flowers in the most frequently used rooms of your home, so that you can best appreciate them. A bright kitchen will look even better with a simple jug of seasonal flowers. A hallway with flowers is very welcoming, and putting a few delicate stems on a table next to your bed is a lovely way to spoil yourself.

Always consider the angle from which the flowers should be viewed – whether from all around, from the side or from above. Make sure that there is enough space around the arrangement.

Any arrangement should complement the size and style of the room. Small displays are best placed in smaller spaces, while rooms with high ceilings benefit from taller arrangements. The flowers' backdrop is also important. For example, mixed bouquets will usually look better against a plain wall than against patterned wallpaper.

Always place flowers out of reach of children and away from electrical goods. Use a mat if you put them on a surface that can be damaged by water.

Flowers will last longer if they are positioned out of direct sunlight and away from any sources of heat or draughts. Try to put them in a spot where the temperature does not vary too much between night and day. And keep carnations and orchids away from fruit or vegetables – the flowers will be killed by the ethylene gas that is given off as the fruit or vegetables ripen.

Glossary

A list of most of the flowers featured in this book and some tips on how to care for them

ANTIRRHINUM

This cultivated version of the snapdragon gives a garden air to any arrangement. Antirrhinums also have a wonderfully sweet fragrance.

ASIATIC LIL

(lilium hybric

Recognisable by its uprigh stem and multiple flowers, th asiatic lily is available all yea round and can last for up t two weeks. Unlike other lilie: it doesn't have a strong scen

CARNATION *(dianthus)*

Available as single-headed or multi-headed (spray) varieties and in a vast array of colours, carnations have a long vase life. Cut the stems between the nodes to help water uptake.

MARYLLIS *(hippeastrum)*

hese striking bell-shaped
owers on a single stem add
rama to any arrangement.
uy them closed to avoid
amage to the flowers.

ANEMONE

Rich colours of pink, red,
mauve and white combine
with a velvety, black centre
to make this a very popular
flower. They drink a lot of
water and need natural light.

ASTER *(aster novi-belgii)*

Sometimes called Michaelmas
daisies, asters come in pink
and white. Considered
a 'filler' flower, it has a
meadowlike quality that
complements other flowers.

ARTHAMUS

his unusual thistle-type
lower adds colour and
exture to any flower
ombination. It lasts well
nd is excellent for drying.

CELOSIA

Brilliant colour and soft,
feathery plumes signal the
exotic nature of these tropical
flowers. Remove the foliage,
as it tends to fade quickly.

CHRYSANTHEMUM

These popular flowers come
in a huge selection of colours
and single and spray varieties.
As long as you remove their
foliage, they can last for up
to two weeks.

FOXTAIL LILY *(eremurus)*

This tall, elegant flower
usually comes in yellow but
can also be found in orange
and white. Recut the stem
regularly and remove the
faded lower flowers.

FREESIA

Best known for their swee
scent, freesias have a fairly
short vase life but will las
longer if their faded flower
are removed. Buy with a
least one bud showing colour

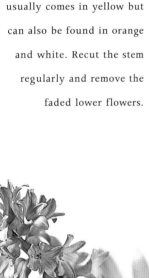

HYACINTH

Popular houseplants,
hyacinths are also very
attractive cut flowers with a
fabulous perfume. Buy when
the flowers are in bud and
cut only a little from the stem.

DAFFODIL *(narcissus)*

There are hundreds of different types of daffodil, including single, double and miniature varieties. They have a relatively short vase life of five to seven days.

ERYNGIUM

Sometimes called sea holly because of its spiky appearance, eryngium ranges from silver-grey to deep blue and mauve. It can be dried for a winter decoration.

GYPSOPHILA

Also called baby's breath, gypsophila is usually mixed with other flowers to give volume. Look out for the new variety 'Million Stars'.

HYPERICUM

This is the commercially grown variety of the garden shrub St John's Wort, prized for its red berry rather than its yellow flower. It gives depth to floral arrangements.

LISIANTHUS

(eustoma grandiflora)
Although this exotic flower looks delicate, it lasts well if you remove the fading flowers. It can be bi-coloured and comes in white, pink and purple.

MONTBRETIA *(crocosmia)*
A garden flower popular for its vibrant colour and long season, montbretia is also a longlasting cut flower. It is sensitive to gases emitted by rotting flowers, so remove lower flowers as they die.

PEONY
Showy, romantic flowers, peonies are the epitome of country-garden style. Buy them with some colour showing and they will last for five to ten days.

PERUVIAN LIL
(alstroemeri
Popular because of i
multiple flowerheads ar
long vase life, this exot
lily comes in purple, pin
red, orange and yello

RUDBECKIA
It is the seedhead of the rudbeckia (commonly known as the coneflower) that is used to add colour and texture to floral arrangements, rather than its flower.

RCHID *(cymbidium)*

lthough quite an expensive
urchase, each orchid stem
ears several exotic blooms.
hey need very little water
d last for up to four weeks.

ORIENTAL LILY

Heavily scented, with large
showy flowers, the oriental
lily is predominantly white
but also comes in a popular
pink variety called 'Stargazer'.

ROSE

One of the top five most-
cultivated flowers, roses are
available all year round. Very
few have scent, but they are
cultivated to last much longer
than garden varieties.

TOCK *(matthiola incana)*

vailable in pink, mauve,
lac, white and cream, stocks
e very popular because of
eir sweet scent. Remove any
oliage from the water, as it
ecays quickly.

TULIP

A huge group of flowers,
tulips come in a vast array
of colours, shapes and forms.
Keep them cool and allow for
the stems to continue to grow
after they have been cut.

index

A

achillea 36

alstroemeria, see Peruvian lily

amaryllis 46

anemones 10, 14, 46, 57

antirrhinums 32, 56

asparagus ferns 50

asters 24, 57

B

baby's breath, see gypsophila

bacteria 8, 9

  cleaning containers 48

bear grass 50

birch twigs 30

boxes 14, 16

bupleurum 24

C

candles 46

carnations 14, 34, 46, 56

carthamus 36, 57

ceanothus 10

celosia 32, 57

chickenwire 8, 32

chrysanthemums 28, 32, 38, 58

colour 52-53

coneflowers, see rudbeckia

containers 48

crocosmia, see montbretia

cutting stems 8

D

daffodils 12, 59

dried flowers and foliage 42,
50, 51, 57

E

echinops 42

equipment 8

eryngium 40, 44, 59

eucalyptus 44, 51

euonymus 28

F

ferns

  ming 46, 50

  sword 51

fir cones 46

floral foam, see foam

flower food 8

foam, floral 8, 9, 18, 24,
28, 34, 38, 42, 46

foliage 50-51

  removing 8

foxtail lilies 58

freesias 24, 58

fruit 22

G

gerberas 20

glass beads 12

grape hyacinths 12

Guernsey lilies 18

gypsophila 22, 59

H

hand-tied bouquet 36

harmonious colours 53

holly 42

hyacinths 10, 14, 58

hypericum 34, 36, 59

I

ivy 20, 28, 34, 42

L

lady's mantle 26

lilac 10

lilies

  asiatic 38, 56

  foxtail 58

  Guernsey 18

  oriental 18, 61

Peruvian 36, 60
   Stargazer 61
lisianthus 26, 30, 59

M
Michaelmas daisies, see asters
montbretia 32, 60

N
napkins 20
narcissi, see daffodils
nerines, see Guernsey lilies

O
oasis, see floral foam
orchids 18, 20, 61

P
palm leaves 50
pebbles 28
peonies 26, 60
Peruvian lilies 36, 60
pine 44
place-settings 20
poppy heads 36
positioning flower
   arrangements 55
primary colours 52

privet 32
pumpkin 38
pussy willow 12

R
rosemary 42, 44, 51
roses 20, 26, 34, 40, 42, 46, 61
   reviving 9
rudbeckia 36, 60
ruscus 46, 51

S
scabious 22
scissors 8
sea holly, see eryngium
sedum 22, 38
stamens
   removing 9
stems
   cutting 8
   straightening 9
stocks 22, 61
sweet peas 10

T
tape, florist's 8
terracotta pots 14, 28, 32
tissue paper 16, 36

tortured willow 18
triadic colour schemes 53
tulips 16, 61
   straightening 9

V
vegetables 38
viburnum 12, 26, 34, 44

W
water
   changing 9
wax flowers 12
wire, florist's 8
woody stems 8

Y
yarrow, see achillea